D1313172

THE ART OF MINDFULNESS

RELAXED AND FOCUSED COLOURING

Michael O'Mara Books Limited

First published in Great Britain in 2015 by
Michael O'Mara Books Limited
9 Lion Yard
Tremadoc Road
London SW4 7NQ

A CIP catalogue record for this book is available from the British Library.

Papers used by Michael O'Mara Books Limited are natural, recyclable products made from wood grown in sustainable forests. The manufacturing processes conform to the environmental regulations of the country of origin.

ISBN: 978-1-78243-503-7

1 2 3 4 5 6 7 8 9 10

www.mombooks.com

Designed by Ana Bjezancevic and Claire Cater

Illustrations by Angela Porter, Angelea Van Dam, Carol Spencer, Cindy Wilde, Emily Hamilton, Fay Martin, Felicity French, Hannah Davies, Lizzie Preston and Sally Moret

Cover illustration by Lizzie Preston

Printed and bound by L.E.G.O., Viale dell'Industria 2, 36100, Vicenza, Italy

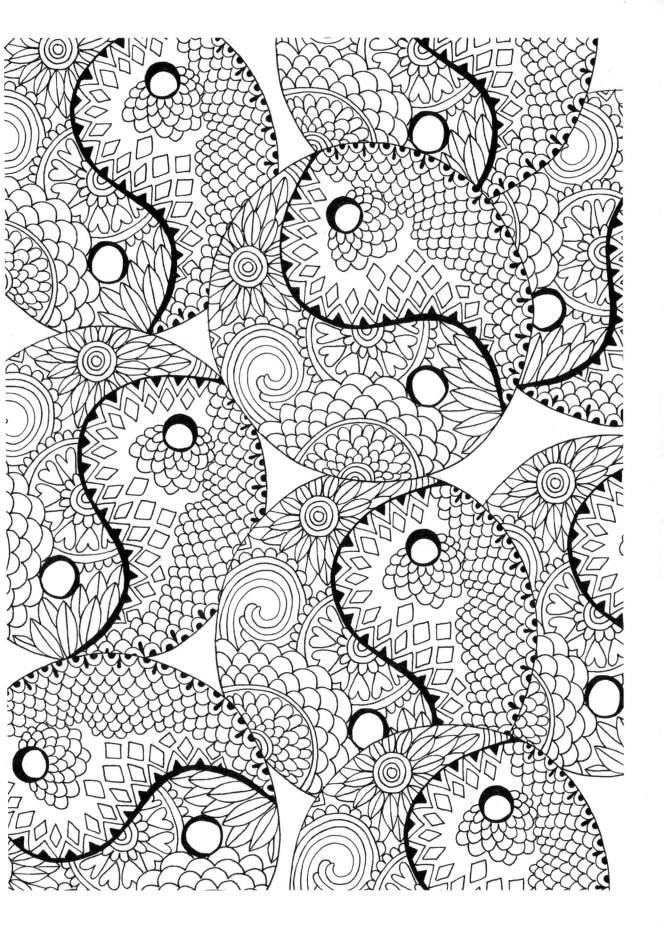

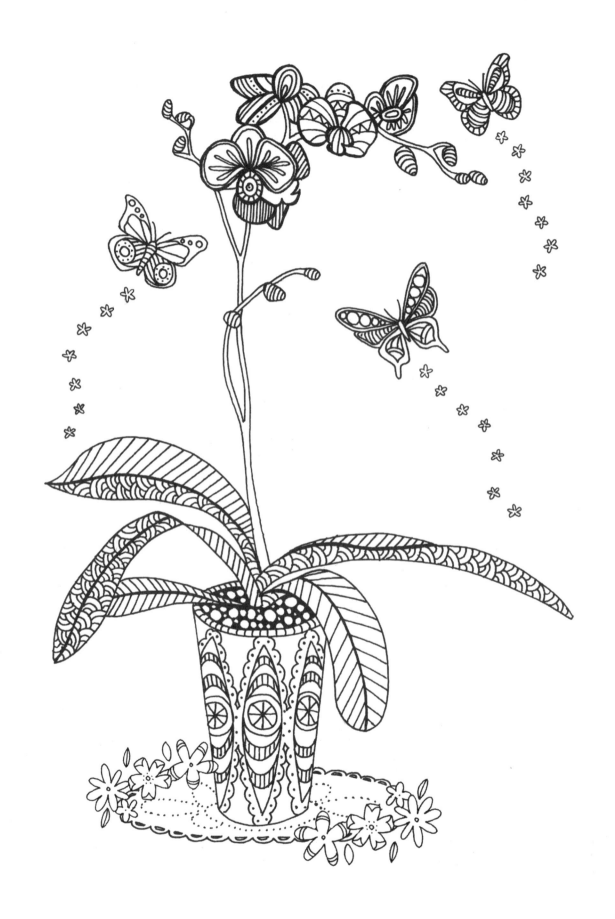

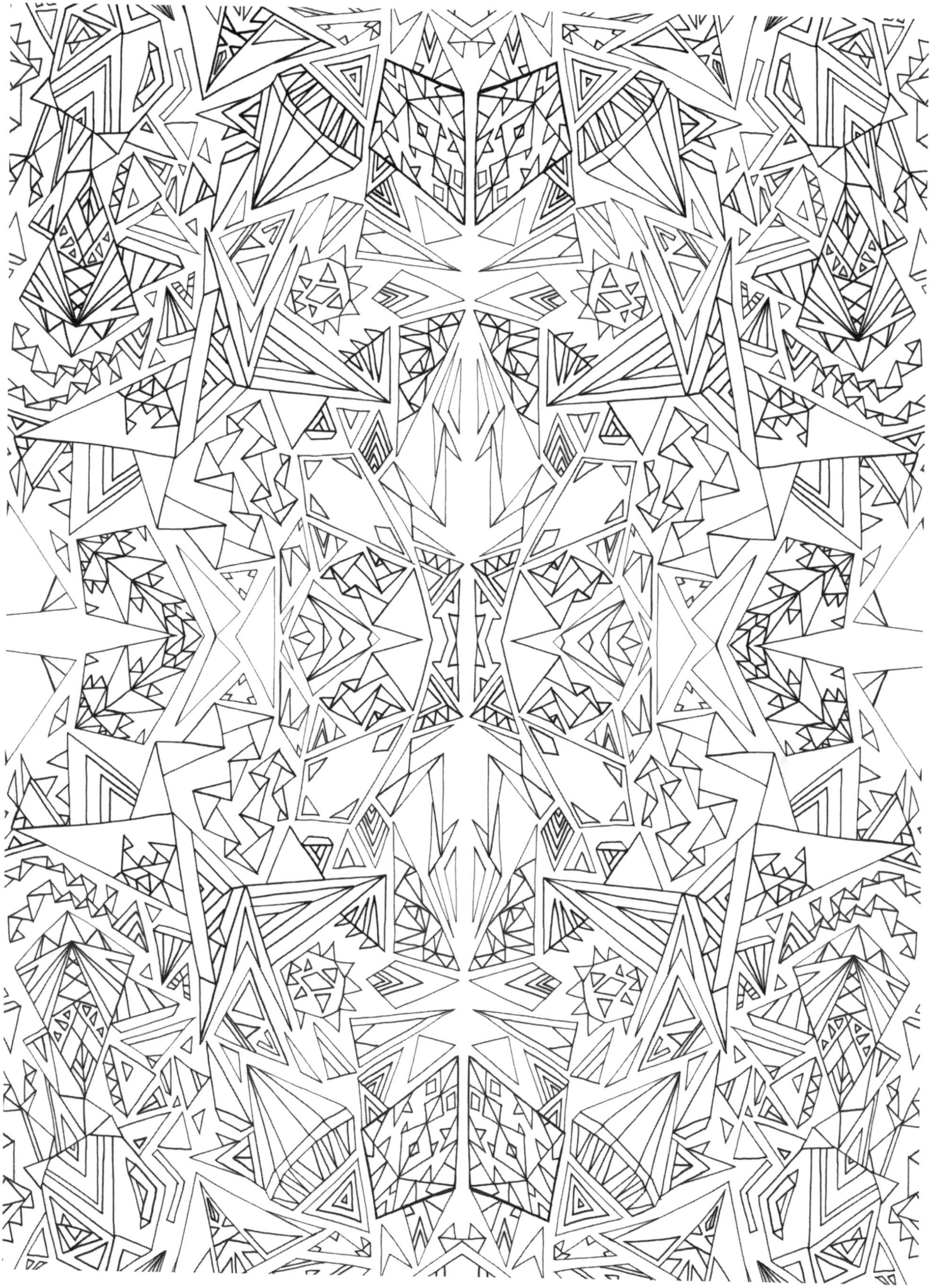

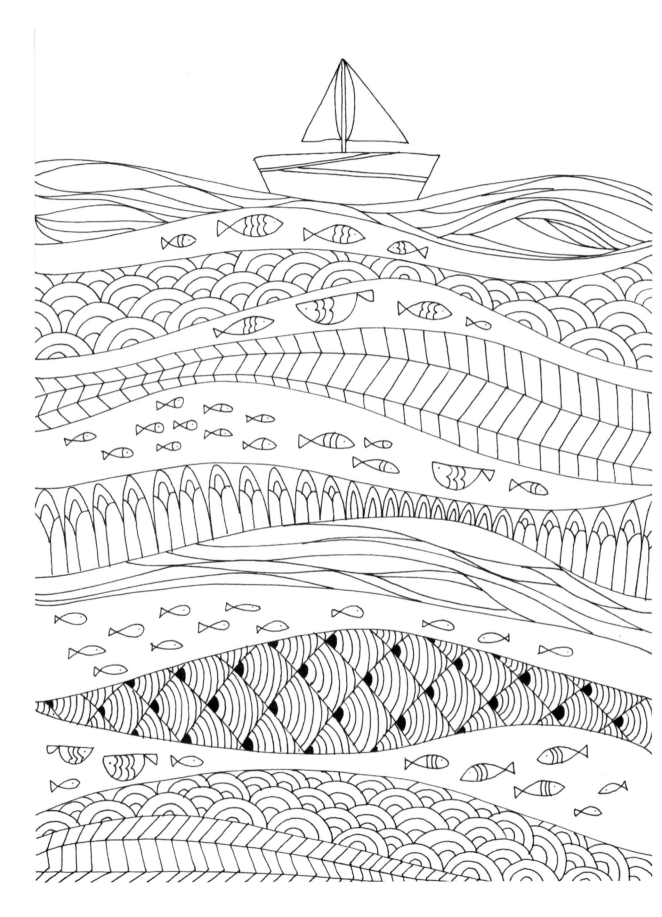

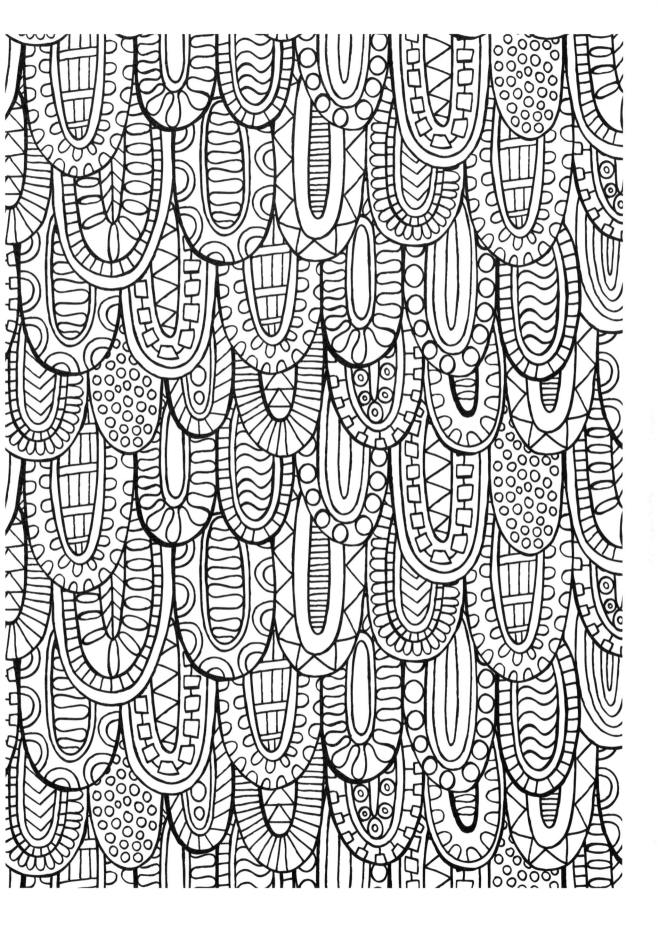